Fact Finders®

STAR-NOSED MOLES

AND OTHER EXTREME MAMMAL ADAPTATIONS

by Jody Sullivan Rake

Consultant:
Robert T. Mason
Professor of Integrative Biology
Oregon State University
Corvallis, Oregon

CAPSTONE PRESS
a capstone imprint

Fact Finders Books are published by Capstone Press,
1710 Roe Crest Drive, North Mankato, Minnesota 56003
www.capstonepub.com

Library of Congress Cataloging-in-Publication Data
Rake, Jody Sullivan, author.
  Star-nosed moles and other extreme mammal adaptations / by Jody Sullivan Rake.
    pages cm. — (Fact finders. Extreme adaptations)
  Summary: "Explores various extreme mammal adaptations throughout the world, including caracals, mongooses,
and bulldog bats"—Provided by publisher.
  Audience: Ages 8-10.
  Audience: Grades 4 to 6.
  Includes bibliographical references and index.
  ISBN 978-1-4914-0167-5 (library binding)
  ISBN 978-1-4914-0172-9 (paperback)
  ISBN 978-1-4914-0176-7 (eBook pdf)
  1. Animals—Adaptation—Juvenile literature. 2. Mammals—Anatomy—Juvenile literature. 3. Mammals—
Physiology—Juvenile literature. 4. Adaptation (Biology)—Juvenile literature. I. Title.
  QL49.R326 2015
  599.14—dc23   2014006945

Developed and Produced by Focus Strategic Communications, Inc.
    Adrianna Edwards: project manager
    Ron Edwards, Jessica Pegis: editors
    Rob Scanlan: designer and compositor
    Diane Hartmann: media researcher
    Francine Geraci: copy editor and proofreader
    Wendy Scavuzzo: fact checker

Photo Credits
Alamy: E.R. Degginger, 9, Ernie Janes, 4 (left); Corbis: Minden Pictures/Flip Nicklin, 17; Dreamstime: Martin
Mcmillan, 13; Getty: Clive Bromhall, 26, Ingo Arndt, 27; iStock: epantha, 10 (left), Mosaikphotography, 15, ThermalX,
11 (right); Ken Koskela, 6; National Geographic: BRUCE DALE, 19; Nature Picture Library: Todd Pusser, 22; Paul
Mirocha, 18; Photoshot: James Warwick, 4 (right), NHPA, 14, Nicholas Smythe, 5; Shutterstock: Anan Kaewkhammul,
7, Anastasija Popova, 10 (right), Anatoliy Lukich, 25, Christopher Wood, 8, Dennis Donohue, 24, Joost van Uffelen,
16, mangostock, 28–29, Sue Green 11 (left), worldswildlifewonders, 20, 23; Superstock: FLPA, cover, 1 (background),
Thinkstock: Lenar Musin, 12; Wikipedia: Cliff, 21.

Design Elements
Shutterstock: Gordan, Osvath Zsolt

Printed in the United States of America in Stevens Point, Wisconsin.
032014   008092WZF14

TABLE OF CONTENTS

CHAPTER ONE

EXTREME SURVIVORS IN A CHANGING WORLD

You see mammals every day. Dogs, cats, and horses are mammals. Your mother, brother, teacher, and best friend are mammals, and so are you!

Mammals are a group of animals that share certain **adaptations**. Long ago the adaptations of mammals allowed them to survive when the dinosaurs died out. Today mammals make their homes where other animals can't. Mammals can be found in every habitat on the planet.

adaptation—a change a living thing goes through to better fit in with its environment

GERENUK

CHINESE WATER DEER

Mammals share certain features. For example, all mammals have hair. They are warm-blooded, meaning their body temperature remains constant even when the outside temperature changes. Most mammals give birth to live young. They nurse their young with milk. Depending on where they live, mammals are adapted in other ways to their environment.

PINK FAIRY ARMADILLO

LEARNING TO ADAPT

Animals may learn new behaviors when faced with challenges in a changing environment. For example, if food becomes scarce animals must develop new ways to find it. Or they must turn to different food sources. Animals that adapt will survive and pass on their new knowledge to their young.

EXPERT HUNTERS

Carnivores are among the most extreme mammals. All carnivores are adapted to be hunters and meat-eaters. Most carnivores have sharp senses and strong legs for stalking and chasing **prey**. They have long, sharp **canine** teeth for tearing meat.

LEAPING FELINES

The caracal is an African cat with an extreme adaptation. This medium-sized mammal eats a wide variety of prey, such as rodents and small antelopes. But its bird-catching skills are what make it extreme. A caracal can leap 10 feet (3 meters) into the air to catch a bird in flight!

carnivore—an animal that eats only meat
prey—an animal hunted by another animal for food
canine—a long, pointed tooth

THE AFRICAN CARACAL IS AN ATHLETIC LEAPER.

THE MANED WOLF

The maned wolf is a unique mammal. Maned wolves are related to the wolf family. This mammal is at home among the grasses of the South American savanna. Tall grasses cover the savanna. To survive in this grassy area, maned wolves have developed long legs. These long legs help maned wolves see over tall grass to find prey and avoid predators.

THE MANED WOLF'S LONG LEGS ARE AN ADAPTATION.

PERIL ON THE ICE

Polar bears are extreme in many ways. They are the world's largest land predators. They also live in one of the harshest habitats. Polar bears are related to brown bears. Hundreds of thousands of years ago, after brown bears traveled north, they adapted to their frozen surroundings. They developed a layer of fat for warmth and a white coat for camouflage.

Polar bears feed mainly on seals. They hunt entirely on ice. Today warmer temperatures are shrinking Arctic ice. Polar bears' hunting grounds are smaller. Some bears may not get enough to eat. Others may drown trying to make the longer swim to land.

WARMER TEMPERATURES ARE SHRINKING THE POLAR BEAR HABITAT.

THE COBRA KILLER

Mongooses can kill **venomous** snakes, even a deadly cobra! A mongoose can avoid most snake attacks because it is so fast. Its thick coat also protects against the snake's fangs.

The mongoose looks like a weasel or badger. However, it is more closely related to the cat. Mongooses eat rodents, lizards, frogs, and birds.

BEST-LAID PLANS

Mongooses come from Africa and Southern Asia. They were **introduced** to the Hawaiian Islands in the 1800s. Farmers hoped they would kill the mice and rats that ruined sugarcane crops. However, the mongoose feasted on the birds as well. As a result, the native bird populations became endangered.

MONGOOSES ARE KNOWN FOR KILLING SNAKES.

venomous—able to produce a poison called venom

introduce—to bring from a native environment to a new one

HOOFED ANIMALS: LIFE ON FOOT

Hoofed animals are mammals adapted to life on the go. Most either run short distances or walk long distances. Many hoofed animals are prey for carnivores, so they must be able to run fast. Others walk hundreds of miles to find food for their herd.

FACT

Hoofed animals walk and run on the tips of their toes.

TOE TALES

Hoofed animals are grouped by their toes. The group that an animal belongs to depends on how many large toes bear most of its weight. One group has two large toes. Usually these animals appear to have split hooves. This group includes cows, sheep, camels, deer, giraffes, and hippos. The other group has an odd number of toes—either one or three. This group includes horses, donkeys, and rhinoceroses.

A DEER'S HOOF HAS TWO TOES.

A HORSE'S HOOF HAS JUST ONE TOE.

GIRAFFE VS. LEAF

Giraffes are the tallest animals on Earth. These African **herbivores** feed on acacia trees. But the acacias try to fight back! In the battle between tree and leaf-eater, some acacias have developed sharp thorns. So giraffes developed a longer tongue. Their tongue slips between the thorns and grabs the tender leaves. This is a good example of an adaptation.

A REAL STRETCH

The gerenuk lives in the savannas of Tanzania, Kenya, and Somalia in Africa.

Its name means "giraffe-necked" in the Somali language. This mammal's long neck helps it reach leaves that are high up. To get even higher, gerenuks stand upright on their hind legs. They use their front legs to pull down the higher branches and nibble on the leaves.

THE GERENUK CAN STAND UPRIGHT TO REACH HIGH LEAVES.

herbivore—an animal that eats only plants

DESERT DWELLERS

Camels are made for extreme survival. They live in some of the harshest conditions on the planet. Desert temperatures range from below freezing in the winter to 120°F (49°C) in the summer. Deserts also get less than 8 inches (20 centimeters) of rain or snow per year. Sandstorms are frequent and violent.

Camels can go a week or more without water and a month or more without food. Most animals, including humans, would die in three to five days without water. How do camels survive? Their humps store fat that can provide water and energy for more than a month.

FACT
A camel's hump can weigh as much as 80 pounds (36 kilograms)!

CAMELS ARE PERFECTLY ADAPTED TO THE DESERT.

That's not all. Camels walk on flat, broad hooves. Their feet keep them from sinking into desert sand. A double row of long eyelashes keeps sand out of their eyes. Their eyes are also protected by a third eyelid. This thin, clear membrane covers the whole eye.

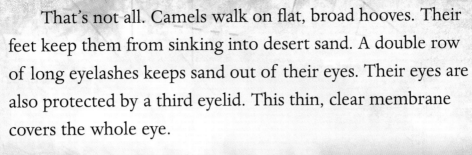

TWO ROWS OF EYELASHES KEEP OUT THE SAND.

THE VAMPIRE DEER

When you think of a deer, what do you picture? Slender, graceful legs? Large, gentle brown eyes? Does your image include long, sharp fangs? That's right. The Chinese water deer has canine teeth. In male deer they grow so long that they stick out of their mouth! Most deer have no canine teeth at all. That's because they eat plants. Canine teeth are usually for eating meat.

So why this adaptation? Chinese water deer have no antlers. This also makes them unusual among deer. Since antlers are needed for fighting, these deer use their fierce teeth instead. Males fight with each other for mates and territory.

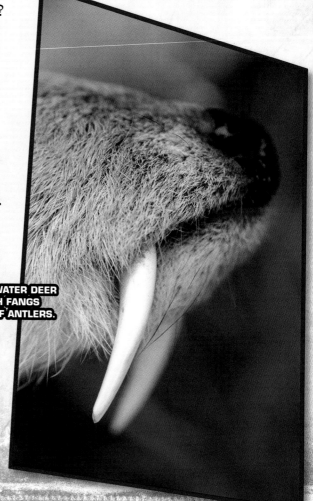

CHINESE WATER DEER FIGHT WITH FANGS INSTEAD OF ANTLERS.

SAY WHAT? GOATS IN A TREE!

Mountain goats are well known for their agility and balance. They have adapted to climb steep mountainsides without a problem. But some goats can climb trees! In Morocco goats can be seen in the argan trees that produce oil-rich nuts. These goats defy gravity as they perch on slender branches to reach the nuts.

You won't find these horned hikers just in tree branches. They can also be seen scaling near-vertical walls of rocky dams! You have to see it to believe it.

AGILE GOATS CLIMB AN ARGAN TREE TO REACH ITS NUTS.

CHAPTER TWO

WANDERERS BENEATH THE WAVES

When it comes to adaptations, few are as lucky as **cetaceans**. These mammals include whales and dolphins. To survive in their watery world, cetaceans have a thick layer of blubber and large bodies to hold in the heat. Water—warm or cold—takes away body heat up to 27 times faster than air.

Whales are expert swimmers. Their football-shaped bodies allow easy gliding. Their tails provide thrust and speed, while flippers help them steer. They have blowholes on the top of their heads so they can breathe and swim at the same time.

cetacean—the scientific name for all whales, dolphins, and porpoises

CETACEANS ARE MAMMALS ADAPTED TO LIVE IN THE SEA.

UNICORNS OF THE SEA

Narwhals live in the chilly waters of the Arctic Ocean. They feed on fish and squid, but have only two teeth. In males the left tooth is huge. It pokes right through the lip and keeps growing.

This tooth is actually a tusk and is made of ivory. No one knows what the tusk is for. Some say it is an adaptation used to fight other males. Others believe it is used to poke breathing holes in ice. Still others think the tusk could help the narwhal sense temperature and salt changes in the sea. The sensitive part of a human tooth is on the inside. But a narwhal's tooth is sensitive on the outside. This new discovery has led to more theories about the narwhal's tusk. Scientists continue to study narwhals and their long tusks.

A MALE NARWHAL'S TUSK MAY GROW AS LONG AS 9 FEET (2.7 M).

CHAPTER THREE

MAMMALS IN THE SKY

Bats are the only mammals that can fly. A bat's front limbs are adapted into wings. Their wing bones are like the bones in human hands.

Bats sleep all day and come out after dark. They aren't blind, but most see better in the dark than in the light. Many bats use **echolocation** to hunt and get around. They emit very high-pitched chirps that bounce off objects and back to their large ears.

echolocation—the process of using sounds and echoes to locate objects; bats use echolocation to find food

MANY BATS USE ECHOLOCATION TO FIND PREY.

bat sonar   returning sound waves

THE WINGED FISHERMAN

The bulldog bat of Central America catches fish! This bat uses echolocation to detect ripples on the surface of the water. Its claws are shaped like fishhooks. They point forward instead of backward. The bat snags the fish while gliding over the water. Its wings beat furiously while its feet grasp the wiggling prey. The bulldog bat can eat even while flying.

THE BULLDOG BAT HOOKS A FISH AT THE SURFACE OF THE WATER.

THE BETTER TO HEAR YOU WITH

The long-eared bat doesn't use echolocation to find food. But it can hear a moth beating its wings in the middle of the jungle. Extreme hearing is how it finds food. The body of a long-eared bat is only 1.8 inches (4.6 cm) wide. Its ears are 1.4 inches (3.6 cm) wide.

CHAPTER FOUR

SLOW AND STEADY

The three-toed sloth is in no hurry. This tree-dwelling mammal of South America may not move at all for hours. In a habitat full of predators, how does it survive?

The sloth's thick coat is made of coarse hairs that are often cracked. In the cracks tiny algae plants are able to grow. The algae make the sloth look like a bunch of leaves. Predators can't easily detect the animal.

THE SLOTH'S THICK COAT ALLOWS FOR ALGAE TO GROW, MAKING THE ANIMAL DIFFICULT TO SEE.

PINK FAIRY ARMADILLO

The pink fairy armadillo is the smallest of all armadillos. You can hold one in the palm of your hand. Most of its body is covered with silky white fur. On its back are tough plates made of **keratin**. This is the same substance that makes up your hair and fingernails. The plates are pink because they have so many blood vessels.

The pink fairy armadillo is found only in a dry, sandy desert in central Argentina. Its extreme adaptation is its enormous claws for digging and burrowing. If frightened, it can bury itself in seconds. Its size and claws help it to do that.

keratin—the hard substance that forms hair and fingernails

FACT The pink fairy armadillo is so rarely seen that scientists still don't know much about it.

BLOOD VESSELS MAKE THIS ARMADILLO PINK.

STAR-NOSED MOLE

The star-nosed mole is blind. But it may have the most extreme sense of touch of any mammal. Each of the 22 fleshy tentacles around its nose is loaded with 25,000 tiny touch **receptors**. They can sense size, movement, and even the texture of objects.

THE STAR-NOSED MOLE FEELS WITH ITS NOSE.

DUCK-BILLED PLATYPUS

The duck-billed platypus of Australia could take the prize for weirdest mammal. It looks like it was made from a bunch of spare parts. Each of these parts plays a role in its adaptation. This swimming mammal has a large, flat tail and dense fur like a beaver. It has a broad bill and webbed feet like a duck. It has claws like a bear and lays eggs like a bird! That's that's not all—its hind legs can deliver a sting with venom. The platypus is one of very few venomous mammals.

receptor—a body part that receives information

FACT

Some scientists believe that the duck-billed platypus' ability to lay eggs shows that it might also be related to reptiles.

PLATYPUSES ALSO HAVE FLAPS OF SKIN THAT PROTECT THEIR EYES AND EARS WHILE SWIMMING.

CHAPTER FIVE

PRIMATES: THE THINKERS

Primates are a **diverse** group of mammals. They range in size from the tiny 3-ounce (85-gram) pygmy mouse lemur to the massive 400-pound (181-kg) gorilla. Primates live in many environments and share some adaptations.

Most primates are tree dwellers. They have hands with thumbs that can grasp tree branches or hold objects. Because their eyes face forward, they can judge how far away objects are. This ability is important for tree climbing. Primates also have bigger brains than any other animals. They can learn skills and solve problems to help them cope with change.

diverse—having many differences or varieties

PRIMATES HAVE THE LARGEST BRAINS OF ALL ANIMALS.

FLASHES OF COLOR

Mandrills are some of the largest members of the primate family. They live in the rain forests of western Africa. They have flowing manes and huge canine teeth.

The stand-out feature of this mammal is its brightly colored face and rear end. Males have a bright blue and red face. The rear end is even more brightly colored. Why so colorful? The bright face helps to attract females. The colorful rump helps other mandrills see the leader in the dark forest shadows.

MANDRILLS ARE KNOWN FOR THEIR COLORFUL FACES AND REAR ENDS.

FACT

When mandrills bare their huge teeth they look scary. But this is really a friendly expression.

THE RIGHT TOOL FOR THE RIGHT JOB

Chimpanzees are among the smartest primates. Many primates can solve problems and learn to adapt to change. But no other animal, aside from humans, can use as many tools as the chimpanzee.

In Guinea in Africa, researchers have observed the chimp community using 24 different tools. For example, chimps use two rocks to crack open oil palm nuts. The chimps hold a nut on one rock while they hit it with the other.

CHIMPANZEES USE MANY TOOLS.

Chimps also use sticks to "fish" for ants. They even fold leaves into "cups" for drinking water!

A CHIMPANZEE "FISHES" FOR ANTS WITH A STICK.

AMAZING ADAPTATIONS

Humans are also mammals and have made some amazing and extreme adaptations. Over time, humans have adapted how they look and live to survive in an ever-changing world.

What are some amazing human adaptations? People have developed advanced brains that can help them outsmart predators, develop new civilizations, and solve problems. Take a look at your hands.

Dexterous hands help you make and use tools. Vocal cords help you communicate complex ideas. Those three features make humans the most adaptable animals.

Humans have been surviving change for thousands of years. Early humans protected themselves from harsh environments with clothing and shelter. Today people build all types of shelters as protection from the environment.

Mammals, including humans, have made some extreme adaptations to survive changes in their environments. They've developed long legs, sharp teeth, and keen senses. Extreme adaptations make mammals true survivors.

dexterous—skilled with one's hands

THE HUMAN HAND IS ALMOST UNIQUE IN THE ANIMAL KINGDOM. ONLY APES' HANDS HAVE A SIMILAR STRUCTURE.

GLOSSARY

adaptation (a-dap-TAY-shuhn)—a change a living thing goes through to better fit in with its environment

canine (KAY-nyn)—a long, pointed tooth

carnivore (KAHR-nuh-vohr)—an animal that eats only meat

cetacean (si-TAY-shuhn)—the scientific name for all whales, dolphins, and porpoises

dexterous (DEK-ster-uhs)—skilled with one's hands

diverse (dih-VERS)—having many differences or varieties

echolocation (eh-koh-loh-KAY-shuhn)—the process of using sounds and echoes to locate objects; bats use echolocation to find food

herbivore (HUR-buh-vor)—an animal that eats only plants

introduce (in-truh-DOOSS)—to bring from a native environment to a new one

keratin (KAIR-uh-tin)—the hard substance that forms hair and fingernails

prey (PRAY)—an animal hunted by another animal for food

receptor (ree-SEP-ter)—a body part that receives information

venomous (VEN-uhm-us)—able to produce a poison called venom

READ MORE

Davies, Nicola. *Extreme Animals. The Toughest Creatures on Earth.* Somerville, Mass.: Candlewick, 2009.

Gray, Leon. *Life in Extreme Places.* Life Science Stories. New York: Gareth Stevens Publishing, 2013.

Thomas, Isabel. *Marvelous Mammals.* Extreme Animals. Chicago: Raintree, 2013.

CRITICAL THINKING
USING THE COMMON CORE

1. Reread page 17 about narwhals. What is the main idea of this section? Explain how the key details support the main idea. (Key Ideas and Details)

2. Reread pages 28–29 about extreme primate adaptations. What is the author's point of view? What evidence is in the text? Do you agree or disagree with what the author has said? Why? (Craft and Structure)

3. Look the pictures on pages 12–13 (the two camel photographs). How do they relate to the text? Explain how they help you understand this section. Imagine you could put any camel picture in the text. What would you want it to show? Why? (Integration of Knowledge and Ideas)

INTERNET SITES

FactHound offers a safe, fun way to find Internet sites related to this book. All of the sites on FactHound have been researched by our staff.

Here's all you do:

Visit *www.facthound.com*

Type in this code: 9781491401675

 Super-cool stuff! Check out projects, games, and lots more at **www.capstonekids.com**

INDEX